HORRiD HENRY'S JOKE BOOK

Meet HORRID HENRY
the laugh-out-loud
worldwide sensation!

....

★ Over 15 million copies sold in 27
   countries and counting

★ # 1 chapter book series in the UK

★ Francesca Simon is the only American
   author to ever win the Galaxy British
   Book Awards Children's Book of the
   Year (past winners include J.K. Rowling,
   Philip Pullman, and Eoin Colfer).

"A loveable bad boy."
—People

"Horrid Henry is a fabulous antihero…**a modern comic classic**." —*Guardian*

"**Wonderfully appealing to girls and boys alike**, a precious rarity at this age." —Judith Woods, *Times*

"The best children's comic writer."
—Amanda Craig, *Times*

"**I love the Horrid Henry books by Francesca Simon**. They have lots of funny bits in. And Henry always gets into trouble!" —Mia, age 6

"My two boys love this book, and **I have actually had tears running down my face and had to stop reading because of laughing so hard**." —T. Franklin, Parent

"**Fine fare for beginning readers**, this clever book should find a ready audience." —*Booklist*

"**The angle here is spot-on, and reluctant readers will especially find lots to love about this early chapter book series**. Treat young readers to a book talk or read-aloud and watch Henry go flying off the shelf." —*Bulletin of the Center for Children's Books*

"I have tried out the Horrid Henry books with groups of children as a parent, as a baby-sitter, and as a teacher. **Children love to either hear them read aloud or to read them themselves**." —Danielle Hall, Teacher

"A flicker of recognition must pass through most teachers and parents when they read Horrid Henry. **There's a tiny bit of him in all of us**." —Nancy Astee, *Child Education*

"**As a teacher...it's great to get a series of books my class loves**. They go mad for Horrid Henry." —A teacher

"**Short, easy-to-read chapters will appeal to early readers, who will laugh at Henry's exaggerated antics and relate to his rambunctious personality**." —*School Library Journal*

"An absolutely fantastic series and surely a winner with all children. Long live Francesca Simon and her brilliant books! More, more please!" —A parent

"**Laugh-out-loud reading for both adults and children alike**." —A parent

"**Henry's over-the-top behavior, the characters' snappy dialogue and Ross's hyperbolic line art will engage even the most reluctant readers—there's little reason to suspect the series won't conquer these shores as well**." —*Publishers Weekly*

"will make you laugh out loud."
—Sunday Times

"**Kids will love reading the laugh-out-loud funny stories** about someone whose behavior is even worse than their own." —*School Library Journal*

"Humor is a proven enticement for reluctant readers, and **Francesca Simon's Horrid Henry series locates the funny bone with ease**." —*Newsday*

"**What is brilliant about the books is that Henry never does anything that is subversive**. She creates an aura of supreme naughtiness (of which children are in awe) but points out that he operates within a safe and secure world…**eminently readable** books." —Emily Turner, *Angels and Urchins*

"**Kids who love funny books will love the Horrid Henry series** by Francesca Simon…Simon's hilariously dead-pan text is wonderfully complemented by Tony Ross's illustrations, which comically capture the consequences of Henry's horridness." —*Scripps Howard News Service*

"Accompanied by fantastic black-and-white drawings, the book is a joy to read. **Horrid Henry has an irresistible appeal to everyone—child and adult alike!** He is the child everyone is familiar with—irritating, annoying, but you still cannot help laughing when he gets into yet another scrape. Not quite a devil in disguise but you cannot help wondering at times! No wonder he is so popular!" —Angela Youngman

Horrid Henry by Francesca Simon

HORRID HENRY'S JOKE BOOK

Francesca Simon

Illustrated by Tony Ross

sourcebooks
jabberwocky

Text © Francesca Simon 2004
Internal illustrations © Tony Ross 2004
Cover illustration © Tony Ross 2008
Cover and internal design © 2010 by Sourcebooks, Inc.

Published by Sourcebooks Jabberwocky, an imprint of Sourcebooks, Inc.
P.O. Box 4410, Naperville, Illinois 60567-4410
(630) 961-3900
Fax: (630) 961-2168
www.jabberwockykids.com

Originally published in Great Britain in 2004 by Orion Children's Books.

Library of Congress Cataloging-in-Publication Data is on file with the publisher.

Source of Production: Versa Press, East Peoria, Illinois, USA
Date of Production: August 2010
Run Number: 13292

Printed and bound in the United States of America.
VP 10 9 8 7 6 5 4 3 2

To the children of
Yerbury Primary School,
who told Henry
such brilliant jokes

CONTENTS

warning!

Do not read this joke book if:
- ☠ Your name is Prissy Polly
- ☠ You're a goody-goody, ugly toad, tattle-tale
- ☠ You watch Nellie's Nursery on TV

These jokes are horrid. These jokes are guaranteed to make horrible little brothers feel sick and parents run screaming from the room. These jokes are so rude and so gross that—

"Hey! Peter! Stop reading right now. I said, put down my book—or else. These gross-out jokes are not for little toads!"

"Mooom! Henry's being mean to me!"

"Don't be horrid, Henry. Let Peter read your jokes."

"NO!"

MUMMY'S CURSE JOKES

Why didn't the skeleton and the monster fight? The skeleton didn't have the guts.

Why was the Egyptian boy upset? His daddy was a mummy.

During which age did mummies live?
The Band–age.

What does a monster mommy say to her kids at lunch?
Don't talk with someone in your mouth.

What did the metal monster want written on his gravestone?
Rust in piece.

What pets does Dracula own?
A bloodhound and a ghoulfish.

What is sung in the vampire production of Abba hits?
Fang you for the music.

Who works in monster hospitals?
A skeleton staff.

What feature do witches love having on their computers?
A spell checker.

What should you do after shaking hands with a monster?
Count your fingers.

When a vampire drinks too much, what does it get?
A fangover.

What did the vampire crawling through the desert say?
"Blood! Blood!"

What do vampires cross the sea in?
Blood vessels.

Which monster ate the three bears' porridge?
Ghouldilocks.

What do you call a ghostly teddy bear?
Winnie the OOOOOHhhhhhhhh.

What haircut do monsters like?
Deadlocks.

What did the pirate get when he hit the skeleton?
A skull and very cross bones.

Why didn't the skeleton go to the party?
He had nobody to go with.

Where do skeletons swim?
The Dead Sea.

BOY: Mommy, Mommy, Ralph just called me a werewolf.
MOM: Shut up and comb your face.

Why are zombies never lonely?
They can always dig up a few friends.

*What do you get if a huge, hairy monster
steps on Batman and Robin?*
Flatman and Ribbon

HANGMAN: Do you have a last request?
PRISONER: Yes, can I sing a song?
HANGMAN: All right. Just one.
PRISONER: Ten million bottles of
    pop on the wall…

Why is the letter V like a monster?
It comes after U.

What did the monster say to his daughter?
"You're the apple of my eye eye eye eye."

What is a monster's favorite game?
Hide and shriek.

What should you say if you meet a ghost?
How do you boo?

What do little ghosts drink?
Evaporated milk.

When do ghosts usually appear?
Just before someone screams.

What would you find on a haunted beach?
A sandwitch.

What do short-sighted ghosts wear?
Spooktacles.

Why did the mummy have no friends?
He was too wrapped up in himself.

Where do ghosts go on vacation?
Death Valley.

GRISLY GRUB JOKES

BELCH!
CRUNCH!
OOZE! SPLAT!
Ha ha ha. These are great
jokes to tell when you want to make peo-
ple feel sick.

VAMPIRE TO SON: You're late. We had
guests for dinner. They were delicious!

What do cannibals like for breakfast?
Buttered host.

What does Dracula like for breakfast?
Ready neck.

Why did the vampire need mouthwash?
Because he had bat breath.

What do monsters make with cars?
Traffic jam.

What do cannibals play at parties?
Swallow the leader.

What does a sea monster eat for dinner?
Fish and ships.

How do monsters have their eggs?
Terrifried.

*What's the difference between school lunches
and slugs?*

School lunches come
on plates.

What do you call someone who puts poison on their breakfast?
A cereal killer.

What do mermaids have on toast?
Mermalade.

Do zombies eat popcorn with their fingers?
No, they eat the fingers separately...

What's yellow and dangerous?
Shark-infested custard.

What do you get if you cross an egg with a barrel of gunpowder?
A boom-meringue.

Waiter! Waiter! Your thumb is in my soup.
Don't worry. It's not hot.

Waiter! Waiter! This egg is bad.
   Don't blame me, I only laid the table.

   Waiter! Waiter! There's a fly in my soup.
I'm sorry, sir, the dog must have missed it.

   HENRY: Why is your thumb on
   my sandwich?
DEMON DINNER LADY: To stop it
   from falling on the floor again.

*What's worse than finding a
caterpillar in your apple?*
Finding half a caterpillar
in your apple.

14

Why don't cannibals eat clowns?
Because they taste funny.

What do French pupils say after finishing school lunches?
Mercy.

What happened to the butcher who backed into a meat grinder?
He got a little behind in his work.

HENRY: What's yellow, brown, and hairy?
PETER: I don't know.
HENRY: Cheese on toast stuck to the carpet.

What do cannibals do at weddings?
Toast the bride and groom.

What do you give a cannibal who's late for dinner?
The cold shoulder.

What's yellow, flat, and flies around the kitchen?
An unidentified flying omelette.

What's the worst thing you'll find in a school cafeteria?
The food.

MISS BATTLE-AXE: Henry, how many bones have you got in your body?
HENRY: It feels like 4,000. I had fish for lunch in the school cafeteria.

GROSS-OUT JOKES

"Out of my way, worm! These jokes are much too gross for you!"

What happens when a baby eats Rice Krispies?
It goes snap, crackle, and poop.

Why is your mouth full of lint?
My mom vacuumed up my candy.

What do you get if you sit under a cow?
A pat on the head.

*What monster do you get at the end of
your finger?*
A bogey monster.

Waiter! Waiter! There's a fly in my soup.
Quiet or everyone will want one.

What's green and hangs from trees?
Giraffe snot.

What do you give seasick elephants?
Plenty of room.

Why do gorillas have big nostrils?
Because they have big fingers to pick it.

What's an insect's best pick-up line?
"Is this stool taken?"

What goes ha-ha-bonk?
A man laughing his
head off.

*Why did the
sand scream?*
The sea weed.

What do you do when your nose goes on strike?
Picket.

How do you make a tissue dance?
Put a little boogie in it.

Knock knock.
Who's there?
Alec.
Alec who?
Alec to pick my nose.

Knock knock.
Who's there?
Ahab.
Ahab who?
Ahab to go to
the bathroom.

What's brown and sticky?
A brown stick.

SCARY SITTER JOKES

warning! Make Sure you can make a quick getaway if you tell a rabid baby-sitter any of these jokes. Believe me, I know.

HENRY: Rebecca, you remind me of a movie star.

RABID REBECCA: Oooh. Which one?

HENRY: The Incredible Hulk.

RABID REBECCA: I always speak my mind.

HENRY: I'm surprised you have so much to say then.

RABID REBECCA: Whenever I'm down in the dumps, I buy myself a new T-shirt.

HENRY: So *that's* where you get them.

HENRY: Why do I have to go to bed?

REBECCA: Because the bed won't come to you.

REBECCA: How long can someone live without a brain?

HENRY: How old are you?

Did you hear about the baby-sitter who acciden-
tally plugged her electric blanket into the toaster?
She spent the night popping out of bed.

Nah Nah Ne Nah Nah

TERMINATOR GLADIATOR JOKES

If you want to make your mean, horrible parents really scream, just tell them one of these jokes.

What do you call a sheep with a machine gun?
Lambo.

What's got four legs and an arm?
A Rottweiler.

What do you call a parakeet that's been run over by a lawn mower?
Shredded tweet.

What did the fly say as it hit the windshield?
That's me all over.

What's the last thing that goes through a wasp's mind when it hits a windshield?
Its sting.

What's green and red and goes around and around?
A frog in a blender.

What do you call a cow with no legs?
Ground beef.

Why did the chicken cross the road, roll in the mud, and cross the road again?
Because he was a dirty double-crosser.

*Did you hear about the man who had a dog
with no legs?*
He took it for a drag every day.

How do you kill a circus?
Go for the juggler.

UNDERPANTS JOKES

Boy oh boy! Jokes do not get more horrid than these.

What's hairy, scary, and wears its underwear on its head?
The Underwere-wolf.

Knock Knock!
Who's there?
Underwear.
Underwear who?
I underwear my mama is?

Why do werewolves have holes in their underpants?
So furry tails can come true.

What gushes out of the ground shouting, "tighty whities, tighty whities"?
Crude oil.

What gushes out of the ground shouting, "Underwear, underwear"?
Refined oil.

What hangs out your underpants?
Your mom.

Why did the golfer wear two pairs of underpants?
In case he got a hole in one.

What's the best way to make underpants last?
Make vests first.

Knock knock.
Who's there?
Icy.
Icy who?
I see your underpants.

What goes 300 mph on a washing line?
Honda pants.

What do you get if you pull your underwear up to your neck?
A chest of drawers.

MINI MINNIE: Do you know how old Miss Battle-Axe is?

LISPING LILLY: No, but I know how to find out. Take off her underpants!

MINI MINNIE: Take off her underpants! How will that tell us?

LISPING LILLY: "Well, in my underpants it says, '3 to 5 years.'"

STINK BOMBS

Hold your nose for these stinkers!

What did the skunk say when the wind blew in the opposite direction?
It's all coming back to me now.

What do you get if you cross a bear with a skunk?
Winnie the Poo.

How do you stop someone who's been working out in the gym on a hot day from smelling?
Put a clothespin on his nose.

Why do giraffes have long necks?
Their feet smell.

What did one burp say to the other?
Let's be stinkers and
sneak out the other
end.
(Ralph's
favorite
joke)

BURP

Knock knock.
Who's there?
Rotten egg.
Rotten egg who?
SPLAT the yolks on you.

What's brown and sits on a piano stool?
Beethoven's last movement.

*What do you get if you cross a skunk with
a cuckoo?*
A bird that stinks and doesn't give a hoot.

What do you call a flying skunk?
A smellicopter.

*What is the feeling that you've smelled a certain
skunk before?*
Déjà phew!

DOCTOR DETTOL JOKES

Next time a doctor tries to give you an injection, distract her with a few of these goodies.

Doctor, Doctor, I think I'm a pair of curtains.
Well, pull yourself together.

Did you hear about the man who swallowed some Christmas decorations?
He got tinselitis.

Doctor, Doctor, what's a good cure for snake bites?
Stop biting so many snakes.

What did the vampire doctor say to his patients?
Necks please.

Doctor, Doctor, can you give me something for wind?
Sure, take this kite.

When is the best time to visit the dentist?
Tooth-hurty.

Doctor, Doctor, people keep ignoring me.
Who said that?

What is the most common illness in China?
Kung flu.

Doctor, Doctor, you have to help me out.
Which way did you come in?

Doctor, Doctor, I feel as if I'm getting smaller.
You'll just have to be a little patient.

Doctor, Doctor, there's something wrong with my tummy.
Keep your sweater on and nobody will notice.

A girl walks into the doctor's office. She has a banana in her left ear and a carrot in her right. There's a piece of celery in one nostril and a small potato in the other.

"Doctor, I feel terrible," she says.

"Well, your problem is obvious," says the doctor. "You're clearly not eating properly."

Doctor Doctor, I keep thinking I'm a bell. Take this medicine and, if it doesn't work, give me a ring.

Doctor, Doctor, this ointment is making my elbow smart!
Then maybe you should put some on your head!

Doctor, Doctor, I've just swallowed a roll of film.
Sit in the sunshine and hope that nothing develops.

Doctor, Doctor, I think I need glasses.
You certainly do, sir. This is a flower shop.

Doctor, Doctor, I keep seeing insects spinning.
Don't worry. It's just a bug that's going around.

DIZZY DAVE'S DINOSAUR JOKES

Dave paid me $1, so I let him add a few dinosaur jokes to my book.

What do you call a dinosaur with one eye?
Do-you-think-he-saur-us.

Why did the dinosaur cross the road?
There weren't any chickens in those days.

How do you stop a dinosaur from charging?
Take away his credit card.

*What do you call a dinosaur with a banana
in each ear?*
Anything you
like. He
can't hear
you.

*Why did the Tyrannosaurus
Rex go to the doctor?*
He had a dino-sore.

What do you get when dinosaurs crash their cars?
Tyrannosaurus wrecks.

What do you call it when a Tyrannosaurus Rex gets the ball into the back of the net?
A dino-score.

What do you get when you cross a Tyrannosaurus Rex with fireworks?
Dino-mite.

What was the scariest prehistoric animal?
The Terror-dactyl.

What did dinosaurs have that no other animals ever had?
Baby dinosaurs.

*What do you call a Tyrannosaurus Rex that
sleeps all day?*
A dino-snore.

*Why do Tyrannosaurus Rex like to
eat snowmen?*
They melt in their mouths.

What's huge and bumps into mountains?
A dinosaur playing blind man's buff.

What do you call a dinosaur with no head?
A Tyrannosaurus Nex.

*What do you get if
you cross a dinosaur
with a pig?*
Jurassic Pork.

How can you tell if a dinosaur is a vegetarian?
Lie down on a plate.

Why did the Tyrannosaurus Rex cross the road?
So he could eat the chickens on the other side.

MOODY MARGARET KNOCKS SOUR SUSAN JOKES

The only good thing about living next door to Moody Margaret is that she knows some good jokes. There's just one problem...

MARGARET: Knock Knock.

SUSAN: Who's there?

MARGARET: Little old lady.

SUSAN: Little old lady who?

MARGARET (yodelling): Little old lady ooooh.

MARGARET: Knock Knock.

SUSAN: Who's there?

MARGARET: Abyssinia.

SUSAN: Abyssinia who?

MARGARET: Abyssinia when I get back.

MARGARET: Knock Knock.

SUSAN: Who's there?

MARGARET: Canoe.

SUSAN: Canoe who?

MARGARET: Canoe open the door? It's cold out here.

MARGARET: Knock Knock.

SUSAN: Who's there?

MARGARET: Bella.

SUSAN: Bella who?

MARGARET: Bella
bottom trousers.

MARGARET:
Knock Knock.

SUSAN: Who's there?

MARGARET: Dishes.

SUSAN: Dishes who?

MARGARET: Dishes your friend.
Let me in.

MARGARET: Knock knock.

SUSAN: Who's there?

MARGARET: Lettuce.

SUSAN: Lettuce who?

MARGARET: Lettuce in, it's raining.

MARGARET: Knock knock.

SUSAN: Who's there?

MARGARET: Sorry.

SUSAN: Sorry who?

MARGARET: Sorry, wrong door.

MARGARET: Knock knock.

SUSAN: Who's there?

MARGARET: Boo.

SUSAN: Boo who?

MARGARET: Don't cry, it's only a joke.

MARGARET: Knock knock.

SUSAN: Who's there?

MARGARET: Abby.

SUSAN: Abby who?

MARGARET: Abby
stung me on the
bottom.

MARGARET: Knock knock.

SUSAN: Who's there?

MARGARET: Nun.

SUSAN: Nun who?

MARGARET: Nun of your business.

MARGARET: Knock knock.

SUSAN: Who's there?

MARGARET: Germaine.

SUSAN: Germaine who?

MARGARET: Germaine you don't recognize me?

MARGARET: Knock knock.

SUSAN: Who's there?

MARGARET: Ron.

SUSAN: Ron who?

MARGARET: Ron as fast as you can!

MARGARET: Knock knock.

SUSAN: Who's there?

MARGARET: Ada.

SUSAN: Ada who?

MARGARET: Ada lot of breakfast and I'm stuffed.

MARGARET: Knock knock.

SUSAN: Who's there?

MARGARET: Cows go.

SUSAN: Cows go who?

MARGARET: No they don't, they go moo.

MARGARET: Knock knock.

SUSAN: Who's there?

MARGARET: Adjust.

SUSAN: Adjust who?

MARGARET: Adjust made a mess on the floor.

I couldn't steal any more of their jokes because...Aarrrgggghhh! I'm getting out of here!

"How come you always get to go first?" said Susan Sourly.

"Because you can't tell jokes and I can," said Margaret.

"I can too tell jokes!"

"Can't!"

"Can!"

SLAP!

SLAP!

BEEFY BERT'S BEASTLY JOKES

HENRY: Bert, why did the chicken cross the road?

BERT: I dunno.

HENRY: There's no point telling you jokes, Bert! Why do you always answer, "I dunno"?

BERT: I dunno.

What do you get if you cross a centipede with a parrot?

A walkie-talkie.

What do you call a sheep with no legs?
A cloud.

Why do ducks have webbed feet?
To stamp out forest fires.

Why do elephants have big, flat feet?
To stamp out flaming ducks.

What goes 99-clonk, 99-clonk, 99-clonk?
A centipede with a wooden leg.

How do you hire a horse?
Put a brick under each hoof.

What's worse than an alligator with a toothache?
A centipede with athlete's foot.

How do you know which end of a worm is its head?
Tickle it and see which end smiles.

What has 50 legs but can't walk?
Half a centipede.

What has four wheels and flies?
A dumpster.

What did the slug say as he slipped down the wall?
How slime flies.

Why did the turkey cross the road?
It was the chicken's day off.

How do you know when there's an elephant under your bed?
Your nose touches the ceiling.

What's gray and squirts jam at you?
A mouse eating a doughnut.

What did the teddy bear say when he was offered dessert?
No thanks, I'm stuffed.

How does an elephant get up a tree?
Sits on an acorn and waits for it to grow.

How does an elephant get down from a tree?
Sits on a leaf and waits for it to fall.

What's black and white and red all over?
A zebra with a rash.

Where do frogs keep their money?
In riverbanks.

How long should a giraffe's legs be?
Long enough to touch the ground.

What's a chicken's favorite TV show?
The feather forecast.

Why do mice need oiling?
They squeak.

What bird is always out of breath?
A puffin.

What do you call a carton of ducks?
A box of quackers.

What's a frog's favorite drink?
Croak-a-Cola.

*What do you call a crocodile at the
North Pole?*
Lost.

*How do you stop
moles from digging up the garden?*
Hide their shovels.

What do you call a fly with no wings?
A walk.

An elephant is walking through the jungle when he sees a turtle sitting by a log.

"Hey," says the elephant, "you're the turtle that bit me 57 years ago."

"How on earth do you remember that?" asks the turtle.

"Easy," says the elephant, "I've got turtle recall."

AEROBIC AL'S SPORTS JOKES

I hate P.E.! I hate Sports Day, too, unless of course I win everything. But Al promised to pick me ahead of Margaret for Soccer today if I let him put some jokes in my book. It'll be worth it just to see the look on Margaret's grumpy, misery-gut face!

Why is Cinderella bad at football?
She has a pumpkin as her coach.

Why was Cinderella kicked off the soccer team?
She kept running away from the ball.

What did one earwig say to the other earwig as they fell out of a tree?
Earwig go, earwig go, earwig go.

What do you call a boomerang that doesn't work?
A stick.

What is a ghost's favorite position in soccer?
Ghoul keeper.

*Where did the Gorilla
play baseball?*
In the bush leagues, of course!

*What is the hardest part
about skydiving?*
The ground.

How is a baseball team similar to a pancake?
They both need a good batter.

*How did the soccer field
become a triangle?*
Somebody took a corner.

Why did the basketball player go to the doctor?
To get more shots.

What has eighteen legs and catches flies?
A baseball team.

How did the basketball court get wet?
The players dribbled all over it.

What kind of cats like to go bowling?
Alley cats.

Why do elephants have gray trunks?
They're all on the same swimming team.

Why is a tennis game so loud?
Because the players raise a racquet.

Why should Sports Days never be held in the jungle?
There are too many cheetahs.

Why wasn't the basketball player invited to dinner?
He dribbled too much.

Why didn't the dog like swimming?
It was a boxer.

What part of a swimming pool is never the same?
The changing rooms.

Where do old bowling balls end up?
The gutter.

What happened when two balls of string had a race?
It ended in a tie.

What's Aerobic Al's favorite subject in school?
Jog-graphy.

JOKES NOT TO TELL AUNT RUBY

Not Suitable for Aunts

MOM: Henry! I've just had the strangest call from Aunt Ruby...
HENRY: Hide!

What do you call a cannibal that ate his mother's sister?
An aunt eater.

What do you call a really old aunt?
An aunt-ique!

Why do you put your aunt in the fridge?
To make Auntie-freeze.

Has your aunt caught up with you yet?
No, but when she does I'm going to need a lot of Auntie-septic.

How do you make anti-freeze?
Hide her nightgown.

How can you tell if Aunt Ruby's been to visit?
She's still in the house.

MOM: Henry, we're having Aunt Ruby for lunch this Sunday.
HENRY: Can't we have roast beef instead?

MOM: Henry! Why did you put a slug in Aunt Ruby's bed?

HENRY: I couldn't find a snake.

AUNT RUBY: Goodness! It's raining cats and dogs.

HENRY: I know. I nearly stepped in a poodle.

AUNT RUBY: Well, Henry, I'm leaving tomorrow. Are you sorry?

HENRY: Oh yes, Aunt Ruby, I thought you were leaving today.

JOKES NOT TO TELL MISS BATTLE-AXE

These jokes are guaranteed to send teachers screaming from the classroom. Just don't blame me if you get sent to the principal...

What did the inflatable teacher say to the inflatable boy who brought a pin to the inflatable school?
You've let me down, you've let the school down, but worst of all, you've let yourself down.

Miss Battle-Axe: Henry! What is glue made out of?
Henry: Um…sticks.

Miss Battle-Axe: Henry! Were you copying Susan's answers?
Henry: No! I was just seeing if she got mine right.

Henry: Would you blame someone for something they didn't do?
Miss Battle-Axe: Of course not.
Henry: Good, I didn't do my homework.

MISS BATTLE-AXE: Henry, I hope I didn't see you copying Clare.

HENRY: I hope you didn't either.

MISS BATTLE-AXE: Linda! Why are you late for school again?

LAZY LINDA: I overslept.

MISS BATTLE-AXE: You mean you sleep at home as well?

*What would
you get if you
crossed Miss
Battle-Axe with
a vampire?*
Lots of blood tests.

MISS BATTLE-AXE:
William! You've
put your shoes on the
wrong feet.
WEEPY WILLIAM: Waaaah!
But these are the only feet I've got.

MISS BATTLE-AXE: Henry! You missed
school yesterday, didn't you?
HENRY: Not very much.

MISS BATTLE-AXE: Henry! If you
multiplied 1497 by 371 what answer
would you get?
HENRY: The wrong one.

Miss Battle-Axe: Henry, where are the Kings and Queens of England crowned?
Henry: On their heads.

Miss Battle-Axe: Henry, make up a sentence with the word "lettuce" in it.
Henry: Let us out of school early.

What's the difference between homework and an onion?
Nobody cries when you cut up homework.

Miss Battle-Axe: Henry! I'm sending you off the soccer field.

Henry: What for?

Miss Battle-Axe: The rest of the match.

Miss Battle-Axe: Henry, what is a mushroom?

Henry: The place where they make cafeteria lunches.

Did you hear about the cross-eyed teacher? He couldn't con- trol his pupils.

MISS BATTLE-AXE: Henry! Why are you doing a headstand in the classroom?
HENRY: You said we should turn things over in our minds.

HENRY: I wish we lived in the olden days.
RALPH: Why?
HENRY: We wouldn't have so much history to learn.

MISS BATTLE-AXE: Henry, I do wish you'd pay a little attention.
HENRY: Believe me, I'm paying as little as I can.

MISS BATTLE-AXE: That's the most horrid boy in the whole school.

MOM: That's my son.

MISS BATTLE-AXE: Oh, I'm so sorry.

MOM: *You're* sorry?

"Henry, I'm warning you..."

"NOOOOOOOO!"

"That's it, Henry. No TV for a week."

"Oh all right. He can put in his stupid, yucky jokes."

PSSt. Listen, everyone, don't read them. They're awful. Skip ahead to the next section.

What's green and rides a horse?
Alexander the Grape.

I thought I said, don't read Peter's dumb jokes!

Why did the picture go to jail?
Because it was framed.

What happens if you fall asleep under a car?
You wake up oily in the morning.

Told you they were awful! Now Stop reading!

Why couldn't the sailor play cards?
The captain was standing on the deck.

How do chickens dance?
Chick to chick.

Groan.

*Why did the man with
one hand cross the road?*
To get to the second hand shop.

Why did the germ cross the microscope?
To get to the other slide.

*What do you call a vampire that lives in
the kitchen?*
Spatula!

How do you use an Egyptian doorbell?
Just toot-and-come-in.

What's orange and sounds like a parrot?
A carrot.

What do you get if you pour hot water down a rabbit hole?
Hot cross bunnies.

You Still here? Then it's your own fault if you have to read dumb bunny jokes.

What do you call a blind reindeer?
No eye deer.

Why did the elephant cross the road?
The chicken was on vacation.

"Peter! That's my joke. I already told it."
"It's my joke! You stole it."
"Did not."
"Did too."
"MOMMMMMMMMMM!"

Why did the bubblegum cross the road?
It was stuck to the chicken's foot.

How much do pirates pay for their earrings?
Buccaneer.

What do you call a priest on a motorcycle?
Rev.

Where do frogs hang their coats?
In a croakroom.

Peter! That's the worst joke I've ever heard. Cross it out this minute.

What did the policeman say to his belly?
"You're under a vest."

What's seven feet tall, green, and sits in the corner?
The Incredible Sulk.

What do you call a bear without an ear?
B.

Only an ugly, smelly toad would find that funny.

What does the Spanish farmer say to his chickens?
  "Oh lay!"

What did the martian say to the gas pump?
Take your finger out of your ear when I'm talking to you.

When is a tractor not a tractor?
When it turns into a field.

when I'm king, anyone who tells any of Peter's stupid jokes will get trampled on by elephants. I mean it!

How do you know flowers are lazy?
You always find them in beds.

What happens when you drop a green rock in the Red Sea?
It gets wet.

Aaarrrgghhh.

Which pet makes the most noise?
A trum-pet.

They're finished. Phew. That was horrible. I'm going to glue those pages together so no one will ever have to suffer again.

JOKES MUCH TOO RUDE TO TELL MOM

yes! Now some real jokes.

What did the constipated mathematician do?
He got a pencil and worked it out.

What jumps out from behind a snowdrift and shows you his bottom?
The A–bum–inable snowman.

A little girl wet herself in class and the teacher asked her why she didn't put up her hand.

"I did, Miss, but it ran through my fingers."

If you're American when you go into the bathroom and American when you come out of the bathroom, what are you when you're in the toilet?
European.

Knock Knock!
Who's there?
Done up.
Done up who?
You did a poo?!

Did you hear about the cannibal who passed his cousin in the woods?

What did the elephant say to the naked man? "You can't pick up—"

"Henry! That's enough! Go to your room!"

The HORRID HENRY books
by Francesca Simon

Illustrated by Tony Ross

Each book contains four stories

HORRID HENRY

Henry is dragged to dancing class against his will; vies with Moody Margaret to make the yuckiest Glop; goes camping; and tries to be good like Perfect Peter—but not for long.

HORRID HENRY TRICKS THE TOOTH FAIRY

Horrid Henry tries to trick the Tooth Fairy into giving him more money; sends Moody Margaret packing; causes his teachers to run screaming from school; and single-handedly wrecks a wedding.

HORRID HENRY and THE MEGA-MEAN TIME MACHINE

Horrid Henry reluctantly goes for a hike; builds a time machine and convinces Perfect Peter that boys wear dresses in the future; Perfect Peter plays one of the worst tricks ever on his brother; and Henry's aunt takes the family to a fancy restaurant, so his parents bribe him to behave.

HORRID HENRY STINKBOMB

Horrid Henry uses a stinkbomb as a toxic weapon in his long-running war with Moody Margaret; uses all his tricks to win the school reading competition; goes for a sleepover and retreats in horror when he finds that other people's houses aren't always as nice as his own; and has the joy of seeing Miss Battle-Axe in hot water with the principal when he knows it was all his fault.

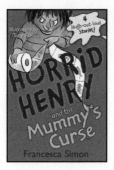

HORRID HENRY
AND THE
MUMMY'S CURSE

Horrid Henry indulges his favorite hobby—collecting Gizmos; has a bad time with his spelling homework; starts a rumor that there's a shark in the pool; and spooks Perfect Peter with the mummy's curse.

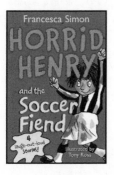

HORRID HENRY
AND THE
SOCCER FIEND

Horrid Henry reads Perfect Peter's diary and improves it; goes shopping with Mom and tries to make her buy him some really nice new sneakers; is horrified when his old enemy Bossy Bill turns up at school; and tries by any means, to win the class soccer match.

HORRID HENRY AND THE SCARY SITTER

Horrid Henry encounters the worst baby-sitter in the world; traumatizes his parents on a long car trip; is banned from trick-or-treating at Halloween; and emerges victorious from a raid on Moody Margaret's Secret Club.

HORRID HENRY'S CHRISTMAS

Four fabulously funny stories that will invoke every family's worst Christmas nightmares, as Horrid Henry sabotages the school play, tries to do his Christmas shopping without spending his allowance, attempts to ambush Santa Claus (to get more presents, of course), and endures the worst Christmas dinner ever!

COMING SOON!

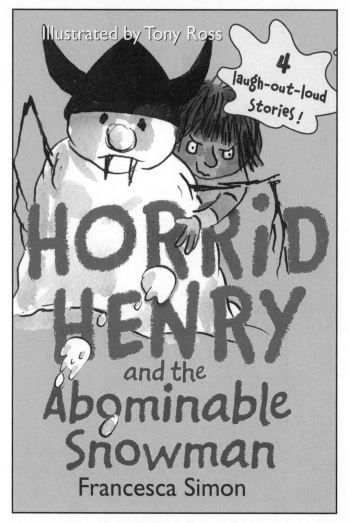

Illustrated by Tony Ross

4 laugh-out-loud Stories!

HORRID HENRY and the Abominable Snowman

Francesca Simon

978-1-4022-4425-4 • $4.99 U.S./$5.99 Can

Galaxy British Book Awards Children's Book of the Year!

About the Author

Francesca Simon spent her childhood on the beach in California and then went to Yale and Oxford Universities to study medieval history and literature. She now lives in London with her family. She has written over forty-five books and won the Children's Book of the Year in 2008 at the Galaxy British Book Awards for *Horrid Henry and the Abominable Snowman*.

About the Illustrator

TONY ROSS is one of Britain's
best known illustrators, with many
picture books to his name as well as
line drawings for many fiction titles.
He lives in Cheshire.